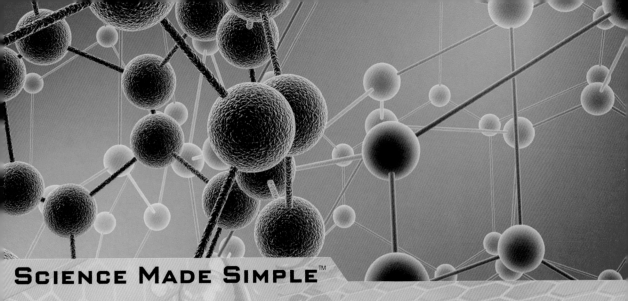

SCIENCE MADE SIMPLE™

ATOMIC AND MOLECULAR STRUCTURE

JOEL CHAFFEE

rosen publishing's
rosen central®

New York

The author wishes to thank Albert Pesant for his invaluable contribution to this work.

Published in 2011 by The Rosen Publishing Group, Inc.
29 East 21st Street, New York, NY 10010

Library of Congress Cataloging-in-Publication Data

Chaffee, Joel.
Atomic and molecular structure / Joel Chaffee. — 1st ed.
    p. cm. — (Science made simple)
Includes bibliographical references and index.
ISBN 978-1-4488-1230-1 (lib. bdg.)
ISBN 978-1-4488-2238-6 (pbk.)
ISBN 978-1-4488-2248-5 (6-pack)
1. Atomic structure—Juvenile literature. 2. Molecular structure—Juvenile literature. I. Title.
QC173.4.A87C43 2011
539'.1—dc22

                                                    2010015454

Manufactured in Malaysia

CPSIA Compliance Information: Batch #W11YA: For further information, contact Rosen Publishing, New York, New York, at 1-800-237-9932.

On the cover: Top: A three-dimensional rendering of a neural network, similar in structure to molecular architecture. Bottom: An abstract image of an atom with six electrons.

CONTENTS

INTRODUCTION

All objects in the world around us are made up of atoms. In fact, all matter in the universe is made up of atoms. Atoms are the building blocks of every substance we can see and even those we can't see, such as the air we breathe.

Atoms are very, very small. They can't be seen by the naked eye or with a microscope. They are so small that 1.0×10^{17} (100,000,000,000,000,000) atoms could fit within a cubic centimeter (.061 cubic inches). In order to see the outline of an atom, you need a special piece of laboratory equipment called an electron microscope. Even then, the most you will see is the shadow of an atom.

The word "atom" comes from the Greek word *átomos*, which means "indivisible," or something that cannot be cut or divided. The idea behind this definition was that if you took a small amount of a substance and divided it in half, and you then took that half and divided it

The central atom is bound to the six surrounding it in this electron micrograph that was generated by an electron microscope.

again and did this over and over again, eventually you would have something so small that you could not divide it in half.

Our understanding of the atom has evolved over thousands of years. For most of its history, the atom was thought to be a tiny sphere. Today, however, it is known that although the atom is very small, it is made up of even smaller subatomic particles called electrons, protons, and neutrons. Just as the atom is the building block of all matter, these subatomic particles are the building blocks of atoms. Each of these subatomic particles has a very important role to play in the activities of the atom.

The world we live in only contains about 112 different kinds of atoms called elements—92 are naturally occurring. Although the number of elements is small, the number of substances that these elements can combine to form is enormous. There are millions and millions of compounds and substances in our world, and new ones are being made every day.

All elements found on Earth are different from each other because each element has atoms with its own number of protons. The number of protons in each atom of an element is called the element's atomic number. All elements that exist on our planet are arranged in order of increasing atomic number in the periodic table. For example, hydrogen (atomic symbol H) has one proton. Therefore, its atomic number is 1. Helium has two protons (atomic symbol He). It therefore has an atomic number of 2. In other words, the number of protons that an element has is always the same as the atomic number of that element. Carbon for example has six protons and an atomic number of 6.

All of the atoms of one element are exactly the same as the other atoms of that element. This means one atom of carbon (atomic symbol C) behaves like every other atom of carbon. Just as all atoms of an element are exactly the same, the subatomic particles of every compound are exactly the same. Compounds are made up of two or more elements, and the smallest particles of compounds are called molecules. For example, the cooking gas in the stove in your kitchen is called methane, and every molecule of methane is made up of one carbon atom and four hydrogen atoms. Therefore, the molecular formula for methane is CH_4. In this book, you will learn about what atoms are like and what they are made of. You will also learn how atoms combine to form molecules.

1

OUR UNDERSTANDING OF THE ATOM

O ur present-day understanding of the atom is sophisticated and very complex. New discoveries are made every year that further advance our knowledge of atomic structure. The model of the atom that we use today is called nuclear, or Rutherford's nuclear model. "Nuclear" means that the atom contains a nucleus. It was not until very recently that we learned that atoms contain a nucleus. For most of its history, the atom was thought to be a tiny ball of a pure element, without subatomic particles. It wasn't until 1910, when Ernest Rutherford conducted his famous gold foil experiment, that scientists began to understand the true structure of the atom.

All atoms, regardless of the element, are made up of three different subatomic particles. These are

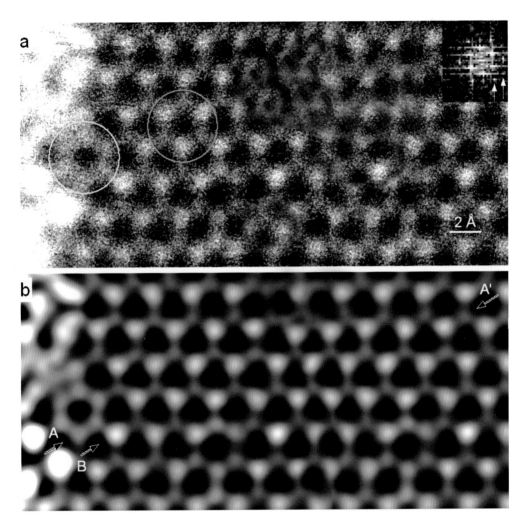

An electron micrograph, which is most often used in the forensic sciences, shows the crystal lattice structure of boron and nitrogen.

the electron, the proton, and the neutron. Each of these subatomic particles plays an important role in our understanding of the atom and how different kinds of atoms form different kinds of molecules. In order to learn where in the atom each of these subatomic particles is found, it is first necessary to know that all atoms are divided into two distinct parts, or sections.

THE ELECTRON

The outermost area of the atom is called the electron cloud. All of the electrons that an atom has are found in the electron

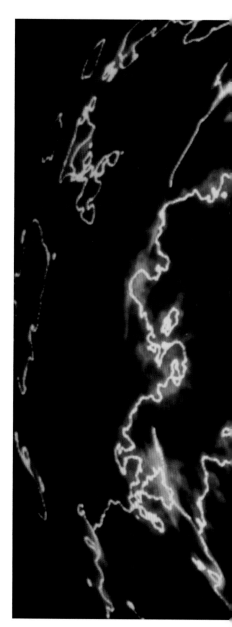

cloud. The electron cloud is exactly what its name suggests: a puff of negative charge, very similar to a cloud of smoke or dust that surrounds the nucleus. But unlike a cloud, it has a highly defined shape that varies only according to the number of electrons in that atom. The electron is negatively charged and has very little of the total mass of an atom, even though it takes up most of the atom's space. In fact, if an atom were the size of a football stadium, the nucleus would be a golf ball in the middle of the field and the electron cloud would fill the rest of the stadium.

A good way to learn the basic nature of the electron is to study the element hydrogen, which contains only one electron in its electron cloud. Hydrogen is the first element in the

The helium atom has an atomic number of 2. Helium is the second most abundant element in the world.

periodic table and contains only one electron and one proton. It is the only element that does not have a neutron. Although the electron is called a particle, it's not actually a single particle (unlike the proton or the neutron) but rather a puff of charge

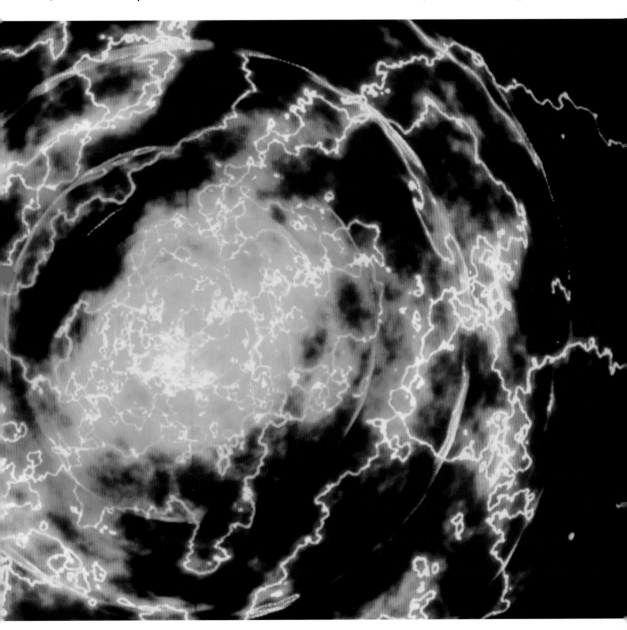

that, according to quantum mechanics, sometimes behaves like a particle and at other times a wave. A wave is a disturbance that takes place in time and space. A good way to imagine a wave is to think of a pebble falling into still water. The disturbance created is a wave. An electron's ability to act as a particle and a wave is called particle-wave duality.

Since the hydrogen atom only has one electron and one proton, it was the first atom that was studied in order to learn more about the electron. From the study of the hydrogen atom, it is known that the electron moves around the nucleus at a very high speed. In fact, it moves almost at the speed of light. Most of the electron cloud is found near the nucleus. As the distance from the nucleus increases, the density of the cloud decreases.

In other elements, or many-electron elements, the electron cloud becomes more complex because the electron clouds can assume more complicated shapes that are determined by the number of electrons in the atom. Electrons repel each other and are only kept within the electron cloud by the attractive force of the charges of the protons in the nucleus. If it were not for the opposite and equal charges of the protons, the electrons would repel each other with enough force to cause them to fly apart in all directions. Generally speaking, the electrons of an atom are distributed among the atom's energy levels, called shells, which surround the nucleus. Each energy level can accommodate up to two electrons. In hydrogen and helium atoms, only the lowest energy level is occupied. The atoms of other elements have as many as seven energy levels occupied by electrons.

THE PROTON

Whereas the electron is found outside of the nucleus, the proton and neutron are found inside the nucleus, which is in the center of the atom and is very small compared to the rest of the atom. The proton is about 1,840 times heavier than the electron and, unlike the electron, occupies a very small amount of space. The proton has a mass of 1.00728 atomic mass units (amu). One amu is an incredibly small amount of mass. There are 602,200,000,000,000,000,000,000 protons in one gram, which is about the size of half an aspirin.

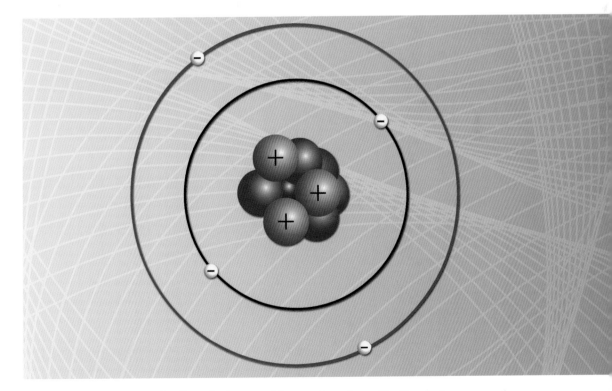

The berylium atom contains four electrons and four protons. In reality, the electrons are not distinct little spheres, but rather clouds of charge that completely surround the nucleus.

The proton has a positive charge. The charge of the proton is equal in strength to the charge of the electron, but it is the opposite charge. The proton has a positive charge, and the electron has a negative charge. The charges of the proton and electron are important because being opposite—like the opposite ends of a magnet—they attract each other and account for the shape of the atom.

The number of protons in an atom never changes, whereas the number of electrons and neutrons can vary in the atoms of a single element. In other words, the number of protons defines the element. Since electrons and protons are opposite in charge but equal in magnitude, an atom is neutral if the number of electrons in that atom is equal to the number of protons. It has no charge. If the number of electrons is not equal to the number of protons, the atom has a charge and is called an ion.

THE NEUTRON

Unlike the electron and the proton, the neutron has no charge at all. But it has a mass nearly equal to that of the proton. This means that almost all of the mass of an atom is found in the nucleus.

Mass Versus Weight

Mass is not to be confused with weight. Mass is how much of something is under consideration. Weight, on the other hand, is the result of the effect of gravity on mass. For example, a dog that has a mass of 44 pounds (20 kilograms) on Earth will have the same mass on the moon. However, since gravity on Earth is six times stronger than on the moon, that same dog will weigh six times more on Earth than it would on the moon.

The neutron plays a very important part in atomic structure. The proton and neutron have exactly the same mass, although they are very different in terms of their roles within atomic structure. Just like electrons repel each other because of their charges, protons also repel each other. Electrons are held in place because of the attractive force of the protons. But what keeps the protons from flying apart because of the repelling force of the positive charges? The answer is neutrons. Neutrons cancel the forces of the protons between themselves without affecting the force that the protons exert on the electrons.

Usually, the atoms of every element have a similar number of neutrons. The average number of neutrons in the atoms of an element is very easy to calculate. Since the mass of the electrons is negligible compared to the mass of the protons and neutrons, generally speaking, the mass of an atom of a particular element is determined by the sum of the protons and neutrons. This makes it easy to determine how many neutrons an atom of an element usually has. For example, most oxygen atoms have an atomic mass of 16. This number is also known as the atom's mass number. The atomic number of oxygen is 8. The number of neutrons is found by subtracting the number of protons (8) from the mass number (16):

$$16 - 8 = 8$$

Therefore, the number of neutrons is 8.

Just as the number of electrons in the atom of an element can vary, so can the number of neutrons. When the number of neutrons in an atom of a specific element varies, the different atoms of that element are called isotopes. For example, carbon has an atomic number of 6, and most carbon atoms have a mass number of 12. This means most carbon atoms have six neutrons. However there are carbon atoms with seven neutrons. Some carbon atoms even have eight neutrons. Their atomic masses are 13 and 14, respectively. All three kinds of carbon atoms are isotopes of carbon. An isotope is distinguished by placing its mass number after the symbol for that element. For example, the symbols for the various isotopes of carbon are C-12, C-13, and C-14.

Generally, the isotopes of every element behave in exactly the same way as other isotopes of that element. This means C-12, C-13, and C-14 all have identical chemical properties. Nearly all elements occur in several isotopes. In many cases, one of these isotopes is more common than the others. For example, more than 98 percent of all the carbon found on Earth is C-12. The remaining 1.2 percent includes C-13 and C-14. The amount of each isotope of each element present in nature is called the isotope's natural abundance.

MOLECULES

A molecule is the smallest particle that forms a distinct substance or compound. Some of the simplest molecules that occur in nature are those that have two atoms of one element combined to form a diatomic molecule. "Diatomic" means that the molecule contains two atoms. A very common example of a diatomic molecule is the oxygen in the air that we breathe. The molecular formula for the oxygen molecule is O2.

Every pure substance that is made up of two or more elements is called a compound. The number of atoms in a molecule can be very small—as few as two or three atoms. Other molecules can be very large, containing millions of atoms. An example of a simple compound is carbon dioxide, the gas

The carbon dioxide gas that is mixed in with this soft drink expands as it exits the bottle. As the molecules of the gas crash into each other, they form bubbles.

that makes soda pop bubbly (molecular formula CO_2). Another common molecule is methane (molecular formula CH_4).

Even though the number of atoms in a molecule can vary, the way that atoms form molecules is always the same, regardless of the size of the molecule. Atoms in a molecule, whether they are of the same or different elements, are held together by bonds. A bond is the link joining one atom to another. An atom can form many bonds. But bonds do much more than join atoms together to form molecules. Bonds also determine the shape of the molecule and the phase of the substance, i.e., whether the newly formed molecule will be a gas, liquid, or solid.

How Atoms Form Molecules

Atoms form molecules when they share a bond between them. Bonds, on the other hand, are formed when the atoms of a molecule share electrons between them. It is important to remember that not all electrons in an atom participate in bonding. In fact, only a very special few electrons called valence electrons can create bonds. Valence electrons can create bonds because of their position relative to the remaining electrons in the atoms of the molecule. In order to understand why only valence electrons can participate in bonding, it is necessary to go deeper into the atomic structure.

The electron cloud of any atom, regardless of which element the atom belongs to, is divided into shells (also called energy levels). The shells are layers in the electron cloud that together contain all of the electrons of an atom. The outermost shell of

The periodic table is a chart that lists and organizes all of the known elements. Its creation is attributed to Dmitri Mendeleev in 1869.

the atom is called the valence shell. Only the electrons in the valence shell are capable of forming bonds.

Generally speaking, the valence shell can hold no more than eight electrons. In fact, almost all atoms are more stable when they have eight electrons in their outermost shell. Since eight is the maximum number of electrons that the valence shell can hold, the atoms become more stable once the valence shell is full. This tendency to fill the valence shell with eight electrons is called the octet rule. Only hydrogen and helium do not obey the octet rule because they have only one shell, and that shell can hold only two electrons. Other elements usually obey the octet rule. Once an atom has eight electrons in its valence shell, it becomes more stable because it can no longer react with other atoms. There is no more room in the valence shell for electrons from other atoms.

In order to determine the number of valence electrons, we must first learn a little more about the periodic table. The periodic table lists all of the known elements. A quick glance at the periodic table shows that the elements are arranged in vertical columns called groups and horizontal rows called periods. Further examination reveals that there are four distinct blocks on the periodic table that are color-coded. The first block, on the far left side of the table, consists of groups 1 and 2. These groups are called alkali and alkaline earth metals, respectively. The second block is called the transition metals and contains groups 3 through 12 (within the transition metals block are the lanthanoids and actinoids block). The fourth and last block, on the right side of the table, is called the representative elements and contains groups 13 through 18. The first and last block together form eight columns and are called the main group elements. Their groups, when put together, are numbered 1A through 8A. In this book, only bonds formed between the first and fourth blocks will be studied. Transition metal elements form bonds in a manner similar to the elements in block 1 and 4, but they follow a completely different set of rules.

Finding the number of valence electrons is very simple. The number of valence electrons in an atom of the main group elements is equal to the group number. For example, nitrogen (atomic symbol N, atomic number 7) belongs to group 5A. It therefore has five valence electrons. Its valence shell still has room for three more electrons. Let's look at hydrogen. Hydrogen has one valence electron. If three hydrogen atoms each share their electron with one nitrogen atom, the nitrogen atom will have a valence shell containing eight electrons. At the same time, the nitrogen atom can share one of its five valence electrons with each hydrogen atom, and each hydrogen atom will have a filled valence shell containing two electrons. Therefore, three hydrogen atoms can bond to one nitrogen atom.

The Periodic Table

The periodic table is also known as the Mendeleev table. It's named for the famous Russian chemist Dmitri Mendeleev, who created the table. Mendeleev was so advanced in his study of the elements that he predicted there would be more elements discovered that would need to placed on the periodic table—and he was correct. In addition to his work on the periodic table, Mendeleev helped found the Russian Chemical Society, was influential in the creation of Russia's first oil refinery, and was a member of the Royal Swedish Academy of Sciences. Mendelevium, a synthetic element, was named after him.

DIFFERENT KINDS OF BONDS

There are several different types of bonds. The simplest is a single bond. This occurs when two atoms share a pair of valence electrons between them. Each atom contributes one electron to the bond. When two atoms share two pairs (four electrons) to form a bond, that bond is called a double bond. A triple bond is formed when two atoms share three pairs (six electrons). Double bonds are harder to break than single bonds, and triple bonds are harder to break than double bonds.

This diagram, which is a simplified model, shows the atoms and bonds in a CH_4 molecule, methane, the simplest alkane.

Bonds usually fall into one of two categories. When two atoms share electrons between them, the bond is called a covalent bond. The most pure type of covalent bond is found almost exclusively between two identical atoms. For example, two chlorine atoms (atomic symbol Cl) share a single bond between them to form a Cl molecule. This molecule has an atomic formula of Cl_2. When two unlike atoms form a bond, the electrons are seldom shared equally. One usually gets a bigger share of the electrons in the bond. Such a bond is called a polar covalent bond. The bond in a molecule of the poisonous gas carbon monoxide (CO) is a polar covalent bond.

The second type of bond occurs when the electron density of one atom is completely transferred from one atom to another. These bonds are called ionic bonds. Ionic bonds occur because the forces of attraction of one atom are so strong that they draw one or more electrons out of the other atom. An example of an ionic bond is found in common table salt (sodium chloride, formula NaCl). The single electron in the valence shell of sodium is completely transferred to the valence shell of the chlorine atom because the positive charge in the nucleus of chlorine is much stronger than the positive charge of the nucleus in the sodium atom. The result is a sodium atom that has a positive charge because it has lost an electron and a chloride atom that has a negative charge because it has gained an electron. These charged atoms are called ions. The positive charge of the sodium ion and the negative charge of the chloride ion are attracted to each other. This attraction forms an ionic bond.

Whenever atoms form bonds, there is a change in the energy. All reactions are either exothermic, meaning they give off heat energy, or endothermic, meaning they absorb heat energy.

Bonds store energy. If a compound is decomposed into its constituent elements, bonds are broken. For example:

NaCl (s) → Na (s) + Cl (g)

The bond between Na and Cl is broken. Energy is required to break a bond; therefore, this process is endothermic. The energy required to break a bond between two atoms is called the bond energy.

The reverse reaction is:

Na (s) + Cl (g) → NaCl (s)

This reaction would give off heat because the forming of bonds is always exothermic. The amount of energy given off by this reaction would be the same as the amount of energy required to break the same bond. But there is one big difference: In the first instance, energy is used up during the reaction, whereas in the latter, energy is released.

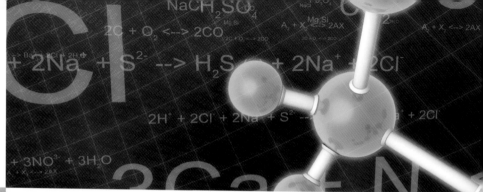

A HISTORY OF THE ATOM

People have always thought about what matter is made of. Several ancient cultures have proposed ideas to describe what atoms could be. In ancient India, philosophers developed a theory of atomism that described how atoms joined in pairs. These pairs then formed more pairs that, in turn, formed substances.

EARLY DEVELOPMENTS

The earliest definition of the atom was developed in Greece by a philosopher named Leucippus and his disciple, Democritus, around 500 BCE. Theirs was the first theory in a tradition that continues to this day. Leucippus and Democritus were the

Leucippus, Democritus's teacher, was the first scientist to develop the theory that all matter is made of atoms.

first thinkers to come up with the idea that all matter is composed of small, indivisible particles called atoms. Democritus proposed that everything is composed of atoms and between atoms is empty space. He added that atoms are always in motion (similar to today's modern atomic theory). Democritus's ideas contradicted the theories of his powerful contemporary Aristotle. Aristotle was the most influential philosopher of his day and incorrectly believed the philosophy of Empedocles, who said that all matter was infinitely divisible and composed of unique combinations of four elements: water, earth, fire, and air.

Aristotle's theory was considered true for more than a thousand years. It wasn't until 1661 that scientists once again took up the study of the atom. In his monumental book *The Sceptical Chymist*, Robert Boyle contradicted Aristotle by returning to the theory of atomism created by Democritus. He advanced the science of chemistry by proposing that all matter is composed of combinations of atoms. This is the view that is held today.

Democritus

Democritus lived in the fifth century BCE. Most of his life is unknown to us, and most of his (supposedly) large writing output is lost to us as well. Democritus is generally considered the first atomist, a school of philosophers who believed that all matter was composed of atoms and the empty space between atoms, which they called void. This belief influenced an early adoption of what would centuries later be called the law of conservation of mass: matter cannot be created or destroyed.

Although Boyle was the first scientist to advance the theory of atomism beyond the basic ideas held by Democritus, the father of modern chemistry is unquestionably Antoine Lavoisier, a French nobleman who was beheaded during the French Revolution. Lavoisier, one of the greatest scientists that ever lived, is responsible for one of the most important scientific concepts in the history of the world. He developed the law of conservation of mass. This law states that matter cannot be created or destroyed, only changed into something else. For example, before Lavoisier, it was believed that when a log of wood burned in a fire, it was destroyed because the matter that the log was made of seemed to disappear. According to Lavoisier's brilliant and radical theory, the log is converted into another form of matter, namely ashes, smoke, gasses, and steam.

Lavoisier also made many other valuable contributions to science. He discovered and named the elements oxygen and hydrogen, making him the first scientist to discover an element. He also helped construct the metric system. Lastly, Lavoisier created the first extensive list of elements.

Later Contributions

For the next one hundred years, great scientific discoveries were made in England, France, Russia, Italy, and other countries. Scientists like John Dalton, who postulated that all pure substances have fixed molecular formulas, and Amadeo Avogadro and others made great contributions to the science of chemistry. However, 1897 marks one of the most important points in the history of science. It was in this year that J. J.

Shown here is J. J. Thomson's historic discharge tube, which made television possible. Thomson ascertained the mass-to-charge ratio using magnetic and electric fields.

Thomson discovered the electron. The importance of this discovery marked the birth of modern atomic theory. The atom was now known to be made up of subatomic particles.

J. J. Thomson conducted three experiments that investigated the possibility of separating the negative charge from an atom, which led to the discovery of the electron. In all of his experiments, Thomson used a simplified cathode-ray tube similar to the one found in televisions before the flat screen. The tube that Thomson used was called a discharge tube. A discharge tube is a simple device consisting of two parallel metal plates called electrodes at one end of it. One of the plates in Thomson's discharge tube was positively charged. The other end of the tube was coated with a phosphorescent substance. Such a substance emits light after it has absorbed energy. When there is a great difference between the charges on each plate, a beam of electricity is produced between the electrodes. The anode has an opening in it so that

the electrons can continue their path.

Thomson's experiment consisted of placing two metal plates in the vacuum tube on either side of the path of the beam of electricity. One plate was negatively charged and the other positively charged. When Thomson turned on the electrodes, the beam was deflected toward the positively charged plate. This proved that the beam was negatively charged. At first, Thomson called the material that made up the beam "corpuscles," but later on he changed the named to electrons. For his work, Thomson was awarded the Nobel Prize for Physics in 1906.

In 1910, another great English scientist conducted research that led to the discovery of the nucleus. Ernest Rutherford, working with Hans Geiger, performed experiments that led to the creation of a new model of the atom. Up until that time, it was believed that an atom's mass was evenly distributed throughout its volume and that an atom's electrons were embedded in a jellylike sphere of positive charge. Rutherford referred to this as the plum pudding model.

The Gold Foil Experiment

Rutherford's experiment consisted of taking an extremely thin strip of gold leaf and aiming a beam of alpha particles at it. A beam of alpha particles is produced by a radioactive substance when it decays. An alpha particle is composed of two protons and two neutrons and has a charge of +2. It is the same as the nucleus of a helium atom. An alpha particle is a helium atom that has been stripped of its two electrons. When Rutherford bombarded the strip of gold leaf with the beam of alpha particles, he noticed that most of the alpha particles went straight

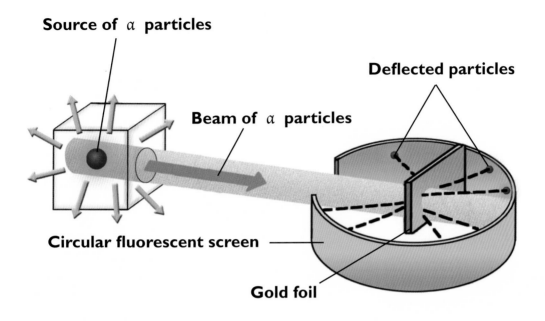

Source of α **particles**

Deflected particles

Beam of α **particles**

Circular fluorescent screen

Gold foil

The cathode-ray tube projects images out, away from itself, and toward the viewer. The tube creates images using a flourescent screen.

through the foil, which is what he expected based on the plum pudding model. However, he also found that a few of the alpha particles were deflected, and some of them even bounced back from the foil. From this observation, Rutherford concluded that the mass and positive charge in an atom were not evenly distributed. If the atom had a uniform composition, the alpha particles would not have been deflected, let alone have bounced back. He concluded that an atom's positive charge and mass were concentrated in the center of the atom and that it was very, very small compared to the total volume of the atom.

Owing to great industrial and scientific design, the basic lightbulb has not changed much in more than a century since it was invented.

Rutherford continued his research on atomic structure and, in 1920, discovered the neutron. He died in 1937.

Soon after Rutherford's discovery of the neutron, the amount of information about the atom and its structure seemed to grow astronomically fast. In fact, it was during the first half of the twentieth century that most of what we know about the atom was discovered. Of all the places where these discoveries were made, Berlin, Germany, seemed to be the center of atomic science. In Berlin in the 1920s, there were seven Noble Prize–winning physicists. Never in the history of the world has one city contained such a high concentration of scientific genius. Scientists such as Albert Einstein, Max Planck, and Theodore Heisenberg invented the atomic science of quantum mechanics.

Quantum mechanics is the science that explores the relationship between energy, light, and matter at the subatomic level. Planck was the first scientist to investigate these concepts and is known as the father of quantum mechanics. In 1894, he was hired by a group of electric companies to create a lightbulb that would produce a bright light but not consume a large amount of energy. The fundamental question that Planck was faced with was: How does the frequency of light emitted depend on the temperature of the filament in the bulb? When a lightbulb is turned on, the filament inside first burns red, then orange, then yellow, and finally white as it gets hotter and hotter. Each of these colors has a corresponding frequency.

According to the laws of classical physics, the filament in the bulb was capable of emitting radiation at any frequency. In fact, these laws predicted that the intensity of the radiation should increase as the frequency increases. While this was the case for low frequencies (red light and infrared radiation), it was wrong for blue and violet light and for ultraviolet radiation. The intensity of the radiation from a hot filament decreases as the frequency changes from blue to violet to ultraviolet. This problem was called the ultraviolet catastrophe. Planck solved the problem by proposing that light was emitted in quanta, or small packets of energy in the form of photons.

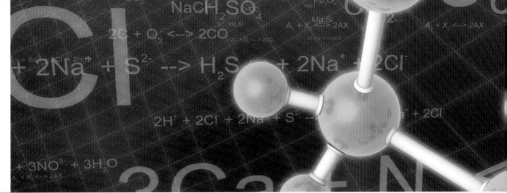

CHAPTER 4

ATOM THEORY AND QUANTUM MECHANICS

At the beginning of the twentieth century, scientists began to explore the structure of the atom more closely. They discovered that the particles that make up an atom did not behave like everyday matter. When they studied electrons, the scientists learned that they sometimes behave like particles, which follows the laws of physics established by Isaac Newton more than two hundred years ago. At other times, these same electrons behave like waves, which obey a completely different set of laws. The great triumph of the theory of quantum mechanics is that it united these two very different behaviors of subatomic particles into one comprehensive theory.

In order to understand quantum theory and how it relates to atomic structure, we must first

THE ELECTROMAGNETIC SPECTRUM

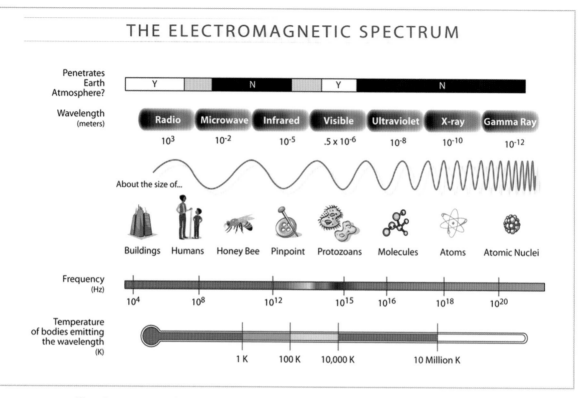

The electromagnetic spectrum is a chart that illustrates the range of electromagnetic frequencies that occur in nature, from radio waves to gamma rays.

learn about waves, light, and matter. A wave is a disturbance passing through space or some other medium, such as water or air. A good way to understand a wave is to imagine waves of water at the beach. As the wave moves toward the shore, the water goes up and down, but most of the water does not move toward the beach. The only reason that some of the water moves toward the shore is because the wave pushes some of the water ahead of itself. Electromagnetic waves are periodic, like the waves at the beach. At the beach, waves rise and fall continuously. The number of times they rise in a period of time is called the frequency of the waves. The frequency of a water wave may be expressed as about five to ten cycles per minute. For visible light, the frequencies are much higher. Violet light has a frequency of 75×10^{14} cycles per second (that's 75 followed by 14 zeroes). Visible light is a wave. In particular, it is an electromagnetic wave. Other forms of electromagnetic radiation include gamma rays, X-rays, ultraviolet, infrared, microwaves, and radio waves. All of these forms of radiation are represented in the electromagnetic spectrum and organized according to their frequency.

At the same time, light is also a particle. A particle of light is called a photon. Like an electron, light sometimes behaves like a photon. At other times, it behaves like a wave, depending on how it is observed. When light is put through a prism, it behaves like a wave. However, from the subatomic point of view, light is quantized. "Quantized" means that light is restricted to countable units, as opposed to a continuous amount. In other words, you cannot have 1½ photons or 2¾ photons, just like you can't have 1½ atoms of an element. Light, when considered as a wave, is continuous. This means that the frequency of light does not have to be a whole number.

THE PHOTOELECTRIC EFFECT

In 1905, Albert Einstein, a friend of Max Planck, used Planck's theory to explain the photoelectric effect. When a beam of light is shone onto the surface of a piece of metal, such as rubidium or cesium, an electron is emitted from the surface of the

Albert Einstein was the most important scientist of the twentieth century. Einstein revolutionized the scientific principles of relativity and unified field theory.

metal. These electrons are called photoelectrons. The energy of the dislodged electron is proportional to the frequency of the light shining on the metal. Most important, the light has to have a certain minimum frequency in order for it to dislodge the electron. This frequency is called the threshold frequency. If the frequency of the light shining on the metal is below the threshold frequency, no electron is emitted. It was also noted that when the frequency was much higher than the threshold frequency, the electron was not only ejected, but it also had kinetic energy.

Once again, the laws of classical physics were not applicable to the photoelectric phenomenon because in classical physics the energy associated with light, or electromagnetic radiation, depends on the intensity of the light, not the frequency. However, a dim beam of light at or above the threshold frequency could dislodge an electron, whereas a very bright light that was below the threshold frequency could not dislodge the electron.

Max Planck

Max Planck was a prominent scientist in Nazi Germany in the years leading up to World War II. He took public stands against the Nazi Party. Planck's son Erwin was executed for being implicated in a plot against Adolf Hitler. During a time of great societal trouble, Planck was a moral and public figure.

Einstein explained the photoelectric effect by assuming that light consists of "packets" of energy that he called photons. If the photons of the light shining on the metal have sufficient energy, they will displace the electron from the atom. If the photons do not have sufficient energy, they will not eject the electron, no matter how many photons there are. In other words, photons below the threshold frequency do not have sufficient energy to remove the electron, and they cannot combine their energies to make sufficient energy.

PLANK AND EINSTEIN'S INFLUENCE

The discoveries of Planck and Einstein proved that electrons could absorb and release energy, but only in fixed amounts. Today, we know that an electron can move from one energy level to a higher one if it absorbs a specific amount of energy. The vacancy created by this electron can be filled by an electron from a higher level. But what happens to the energy of that electron when it drops to a lower energy level? The answer is that the electron releases this extra energy in the form of a photon. This is the basic principle behind the neon lamp. As the current goes through the neon gas, atoms of neon absorb energy, and some of the electrons absorb energy. These high-energy electrons return to lower energy, and light is given off in the form of photons. The photons have energies that correspond to the energy of red and orange light. This is why the neon tube has its red-orange color.

A few years before Planck and Einstein completed their work, other scientists had already been studying emissions spectra. An emission spectrum of an element is a set of colors of light emitted by the atoms of that element as the excited electrons return to ground state. Compounds also have emission spectra. The first element whose emission spectrum was studied was hydrogen. In 1885, Johann Balmer developed a formula for determining the frequency of each emission. Today, these spectra are called the Balmer series in his honor.

But why are these spectra important? Excited atoms give off energy when they return to their ground state. Every photon that is emitted has a specific frequency, and the spectra that correspond to each element or compound can be explained

Niels Bohr, one of the most influential physicists that ever lived, developed the theory that electrons move in orbits and around the nucleus of an atom.

by concluding that only unique energy states are possible for the atoms of every element and that the emitted photons correspond to the difference between these states.

It wasn't until 1913, however, that a theory was developed to explain the atomic spectrum of hydrogen. It was at this point that Niels Bohr, a Danish physicist, explained that the electron traveled around the nucleus of an atom, much like the planets orbit the sun. He also suggested that when an electron absorbs energy, it jumps into a higher orbit that is farther away from the nucleus. We now know that this model is incorrect, but it was nevertheless a tremendous achievement because it allowed Bohr to calculate the wavelengths of the emission spectrum of hydrogen with amazing accuracy. For his work, Bohr was awarded the Nobel Prize in Physics in 1922.

SPLITTING THE ATOM

O ur knowledge of atomic structure has allowed us to harness the energy contained in the atom for many useful purposes. Today, hundreds of cities around the globe are powered by nuclear power plants. Dozens of submarines under the oceans of the world never need to be refueled. Every day, cancer patients and other sick people are healed with radiation therapy. All of these forms of energy are derived from the nucleus of atoms.

Nuclear energy was born in 1905, when Albert Einstein published "On the Electrodynamics of Moving Bodies." In this paper, he included one of the most famous equations in the world:

$$E = mc^2$$

Shown is the cooling column of a nuclear reactor. The steam rising above the column is the result of water cooling the reaction chamber. Without it, the reactor would experience a meltdown.

The meaning of this formula is that mass and energy are equivalent. When Einstein published his paper, very few scientists accepted the idea that matter could be converted into energy. Part of this response was due to the belief in the law of conservation of mass.

In this formula, "E" stands for energy, "m" stands for mass, and "c" stands for the speed of light. The speed of light is 299,792,458 meters per second, which is about 186,000 miles per second (300,000 kilometers per second). At that speed, a beam of light could go around the equator more than seven times in one second. That's pretty fast. But in terms of our equation, the significance is that a tiny amount of matter could yield a vast amount of energy.

FISSION

How does nuclear energy work? Protons and neutrons are held together by binding energy. Binding energy is in many ways similar to bond energy. In the same way that bond energy is the amount of energy required to break a bond, binding energy is the amount of energy needed to dissociate a nucleus into protons and neutrons. It is equal in magnitude to the amount of energy released when the nucleus is formed from neutrons and protons.

Fission is the splitting of a nucleus into two or more lighter, or smaller, nuclei. This splitting is accompanied by the release of a great deal of energy. However, only a few nuclei can undergo fission. The most common fissionable material is uranium-235. The number 235 refers to the specific isotope of uranium that is most commonly used in fission reactions. The fission of uranium-235 is triggered by the conversion of uranium-235 into uranium 236. The extra amu is the result of the addition of a neutron to the nucleus. The nucleus at this point begins to fall apart because it has too many neutrons. The result is two nuclei with masses of about 140 and 90 amu. The uranium-235 nucleus can disintegrate in different sets of nuclei, such as Kr-92 and Ba-141. Another possibility is Sr-90 and Xe-144.

As the nucleus disintegrates, it gives off more neutrons than it consumes. These loose neutrons can have enough energy to smash other uranium nuclei that, in turn, undergo fission and release more nuclei. The result is a self-sustained chain of reactions called the nuclear chain reaction. This string of events liberates a tremendous amount of energy. In fact, a pellet of uranium the size of an aspirin can release as much energy as 3.4 barrels of crude oil.

Because a uranium-234 nucleus releases more neutrons than it consumes, this reaction can rapidly increase in speed and become uncontrollable. For a fission reaction to occur at

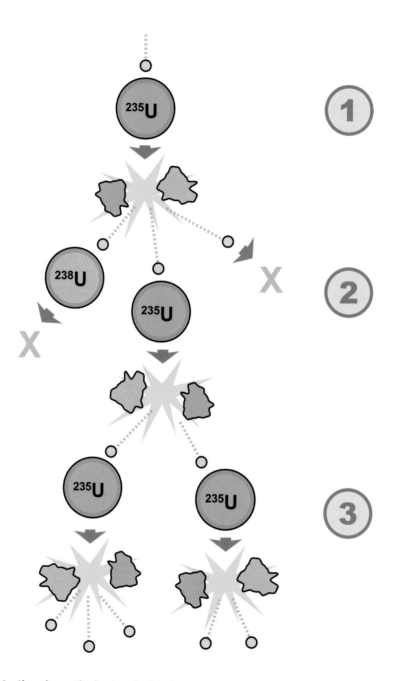

This illustration shows the basic principle behind nuclear fission. An atom of U-235 smashes into another atom of U-235. Protons and neutrons, released at high speeds, collide with other U-235 atoms.

a constant rate, conditions have to be carefully controlled. Many factors are involved. The concentration of the fissionable material and the mass of the sample has a direct effect on whether the reaction will lead to a nuclear chain reaction or not. In fact, even the shape of the sample can affect the success of the reaction. However, the most important factor is the mass of the sample. A minimum amount of the fissionable material is required. This is called the critical mass. If the sample is too small, the neutrons generated by the initial fission will escape from the sample and not start the fissioning of another nucleus. If the sample is too large, the neutrons will split other nuclei too quickly and the result will be an explosion. This is the principle behind atomic bombs.

In a nuclear reactor, the most common nuclear fuel is a pellet of uranium containing about 3 percent uranium-235. If the pellet contains more than about 9 percent, an explosion will result. Besides explosions, other problems are often encountered in the operation of a nuclear power plant. When uranium is mined, less than 1 percent of the ore contains the fissionable isotope U-235. In order to make uranium usable, it

Mass

It was once believed that mass could not be created or destroyed, only converted into another form of mass. While it is true that matter cannot be created or destroyed, it can be converted into energy. But even here, whenever a chemical reaction takes place, an undetectable change in mass will take place.

must undergo the costly process of enrichment. After the reaction has taken place, the waste product is extremely toxic and must be reprocessed and stored. The waste product can remain dangerous for thousands of years. Lastly, there is the problem of eventual shortage, similar to fossil fuel.

HOW A NUCLEAR REACTOR WORKS

In a nuclear reactor, the nuclear reaction takes place in the reactor core. Fuel rods containing enriched uranium dioxide (UO_2) are inserted into the reactor core. Uranium has to be enriched because the 3 percent of the uranium used in nuclear reactors must be the U-235 isotope. This isotope has a natural abundance of only 0.7 percent. The rod inserted into the core must have a concentration of at least 3 percent, but not higher than about 9 percent. This amount is crucial because it is the only way to keep the fission process and reaction under control. The fission rate is kept under control with control rods. These rods contain neutron-absorbing atoms such as cadmium (atomic symbol Cd) or boron (atomic symbol B). The reaction rate is increased by raising the control rods out of the core. By the same token, the reaction rate is decreased by lowering the control rods into the core. The reaction can even be stopped by fully lowering the control rods into the core.

It is of paramount importance that there be just enough neutrons to keep the reaction self-sustaining. If there are too few neutrons, the reaction will die out. Too many neutrons and the core will overheat and the plant will undergo meltdown. In order to control the speed of the neutrons through

The Chernobyl nuclear reactor meltdown was one of the worst nuclear accidents in history. Clean-up workers, like those shown here, are still experiencing the painful consequences of exposure to nuclear material.

the fuel rods, a moderator must be present. A moderator is a substance whose molecules interfere with the chain reaction by colliding with the neutrons released from a nucleus. Common moderators are water, graphite (a form of carbon), and heavy water. Graphite has the distinct disadvantage of being combustible. In fact, the Chernobyl disaster in Ukraine in 1986 came about because the graphite in the reactor caught fire in addition to human error. The release of radioactive waste product into the environment required the evacuation of thousands of people. Thirty-one people died in the accident, and it is expected that tens of thousands of others will develop radiation-induced cancers for years to come.

A nuclear chain reaction takes place in a sealed chamber filled with a circulating fluid. The fluid is pumped through a circuit of pipes inside the hot reactor, and the fluid absorbs the heat. The fluid then flows through water, causing the water to boil. The steam from the boiling water runs a steam turbine. The turbine is connected to an electric generator, and electricity is produced.

FUSION

Whereas fission is the splitting of atoms, fusion is the exothermic combination of light nuclei to form a heavy nucleus. In order for fusion to occur, the nuclei of the atoms being fused must collide at very high speeds. Very high temperatures and pressures are required to fuse these nuclei. Many scientists believe that fusion may be the best choice for the production of energy in the future. Because of the high temperature that is required to fuse nuclei, fusion reactions are also called thermonuclear reactions.

Nuclear fusion is the source of all the elements in the universe, which is expanding. Because we know the rate at which it is expanding, we know that the Big Bang occurred about fifteen billion years ago. About three minutes after the Big Bang, the temperature of the universe was about 1,000,000,000 degrees kelvin. At this point, the universe was a hot soup called plasma. As it began to cool, protons began to fuse and form the nuclei of elements. The first elements to form were isotopes of hydrogen and helium. Five hundred thousand years after the Big Bang, the temperature of the universe was about 4,000 degrees kelvin and heavier elements had not yet formed. At this point, the universe was filled with giant clouds of hydrogen and helium. Some of these clouds were denser than others. The gravitational forces between them drew them together to form galaxies and stars. Today, we know that almost all of the elements known to man are produced in the deep layers of large stars where the temperature is hot enough to sustain fusion.

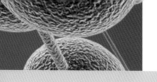

GLOSSARY

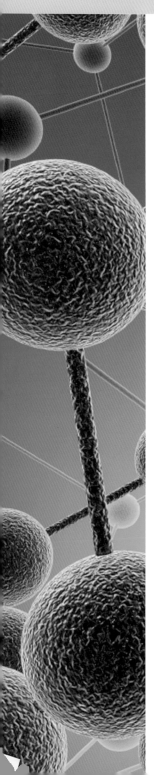

alpha particle The nucleus of a helium-4 atom, i.e., one that contains two protons and two neutrons.

atom The smallest particle of an element, which contains negatively charged electrons surrounding a positively charged nucleus.

atomic mass number The sum of the numbers of protons and neutrons in the nucleus of an atom.

atomic number The number of protons in the nucleus of an atom.

binding energy The energy required to decompose a nucleus into protons and neutrons.

bond The force that holds two atoms together.

compound A substance composed of two or more elements in a fixed, unchangeable ratio.

electron A negatively charged particle found in the space outside the nucleus of an atom.

electron cloud The space occupied by an electron surrounding an atom.

element A substance whose atoms are identical.

enrichment The process of increasing the amount of a specific isotope in nuclear fuel.

fission The splitting of the nucleus of an atom into two smaller nuclei.

frequency The number of times something happens within a given time.

fusion The merging of two or more nuclei to form a heavier nucleus.

ion An atom or group of bonded atoms that has an electrical charge, either positive or negative. If the ion has more protons than electrons, it will be positively charged. If it has more electrons than protons, it will be negatively charged.

isotope An atom with the same atomic number but a different mass number.

kinetic energy The energy that an object has as a result of its movement or motion.

magnitude The size of something.

mass A property of matter that expresses the amount of a substance.

octet rule A description of how the valence electrons in bonded atoms interact so that each atom has a filled valence shell of usually eight electrons.

periodic table A list of elements organized according to atomic number and properties.

phase The state that something is found in. There are three phases: gas, liquid, and solid.

proton A positively charged particle found in the nucleus of all atoms.

radiation The emission or propagation of waves or particles. Common forms of radiation include light, radio waves, and X-rays.

valence electron An electron found in an atom's outermost shell or energy level.

wave A periodic disturbance passing through a medium, such as air or water. The number of cycles the wave passes at a given point is called the wave's frequency.

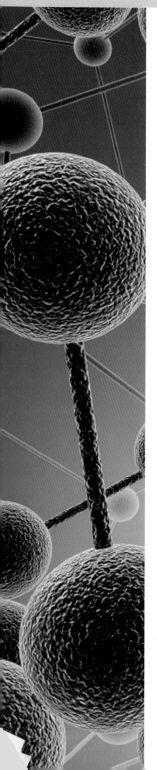

FOR MORE INFORMATION

American Association for the Advancement of Science (AAAS)
1200 New York Avenue NW
Washington, DC 20005
(202) 326-6400
Web site: http://www.aaas.org
The association's Web site offers articles from *Science Weekly* and a wide selection of writings about science and law, as well as membership information.

American Chemical Society: Science for Kids (ACS)
1155 Sixteenth Street NW
Washington, DC 20036
(800) 227-5558
Web site: http://www.acs.org
The ACS Web site's "Science for Kids" section is filled with fun, educational activities on issues such as motion and energy, chemical and physical change, and the characteristics of materials.

Chemical Institute of Canada (CIC)
130 Slater Street, Suite 550
Ottawa, ON K1P 6E2
Canada
(888) 542-2242

Web site: http://www.cheminst.ca

The CIC oversees several societies, including the Society for Chemistry, Society for Chemical Engineering, and Society for Chemical Technology. Its Web site has a variety of information about the organization and its work.

NASA Kid's Club

Public Communications Office

NASA Headquarters, Suite 5K39

Washington, DC 20546-0001

(202) 358-0001

Web site: http://kids.msfc.nasa.gov

NASA's Kid's Club is an interactive Web site featuring news, a treasure trove of pictures, and an "Explore with Us" game section.

National Academy of Sciences

500 Fifth Street NW

Washington, DC 20001

(202) 334-2000

Web site: http://www.nasonline.org

The National Academy of Sciences' Web site contains much information, including issues of its scientific journal, videos from conventions, and podcasts.

National Science Foundation (NSF)

4201 Wilson Boulevard

Arlington, VA 22230

(703) 292-51111

Web site: http://www.nsf.gov

Full of information about funding and awards, the NSF's Web site fulfills its federal obligation "to promote the progress of science." Other education materials are also available.

Youth Science Canada
P.O. Box 523, Station R
Toronto, ON M4G 4E1
Canada
(866) 341-0040
Web site: http://www.ysf.ca
A volunteer organization, Youth Science Canada promotes excellence in the field of science. Its Web site features educational materials, as well as information about membership and volunteer opportunities.

WEB SITES

Due to the changing nature of Internet links, Rosen Publishing has developed an online list of Web sites related to the subject of this book. This site is updated regularly. Please use this link to access the list:

http://www.rosenlinks.com/sms/aams

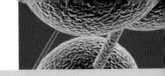

FOR FURTHER READING

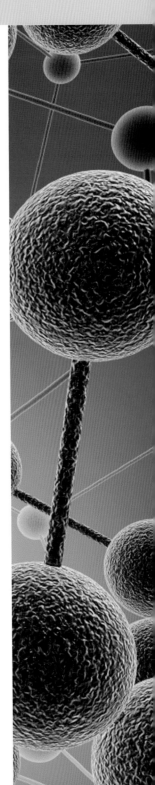

Aloian, Molly. *Atoms and Molecules*. New York, NY: Crabtree, 2009.

Basher, Simon, and Adrian Dingle. *The Periodic Table*. New York, NY: Paw Prints, 2007.

Basher, Simon, and Dan Green. *Physics: Why It Matters*. New York, NY: Kingfisher, 2008.

Bradley, Kimberly Brubaker, and Paul Meisel. *Energy Makes Things Happen*. New York, NY, HarperCollins: 2003.

Brown, Cynthia Light, and Blair Shedd. *Amazing Kitchen Chemistry Projects You Can Build Yourself*. Chicago, IL: Nomad Press, 2008.

Cherkas, Andrew. *Advantage Chemistry*. Markham, ON, Canada: Fitzhenry & Whiteside, 2005.

Cleave, Janice Van. *Energy for Every Kid: Easy Activities That Make Learning Science Fun*. Hoboken, NJ: Wiley, 2005.

Cromie, Robert. *The Crack of Doom*. London, England: Kessinger Publishing, 2007.

Farndon, John. *Chemicals*. Tarrytown, NY: Benchmark Books, 2003.

Garbot, Dave, and Louis V. Loeschnig. *Chemistry Experiments*. New York, NY: Sterling Publishing, 2005.

Hickam, Homer H. *Rocket Boys: A Memoir*. New York, NY: Delacorte Press, 1998.

LaBaff, Tom, Veronika Alice Gunter, and Joe Rhatigan. *Cool Chemistry Concoctions: 50*

Formulas That Fizz, Foam, Splatter & Ooze. New York, NY: Lark Books, 2005.

McMonagle, Derek. *Chemistry: An Illustrated Guide to Science*. New York, NY: Chelsea House, 2006.

Meisel, Paul, and Kathleen Weidner Zoehfeld. *What Is the World Made Of?: All About Solids, Liquids, and Gases*. New York, NY: HarperCollins, 2009.

Miller, Ron. *The Elements: What You Really Want to Know*. Minneapolis, MN. Twenty-First Century Books, 2006.

Newmark, Ann. *Chemistry*. New York, NY: DK Publishing, 2005.

Oxlade, Chris. *Atoms*. Oxford, England: Heinemann Library, 2008.

Sussman, Art. *Dr. Art's Guide to Science: Connecting Atoms, Galaxies, and Everything in Between*. San Francisco, CA: Josey-Bass, 2006.

Vonnegut, Kurt. *Cat's Cradle*. New York, NY: Delacorte Press, 1963.

Winston, Robert M. K. *It's Elementary*. New York, NY: DK Publishing, 2007.

BIBLIOGRAPHY

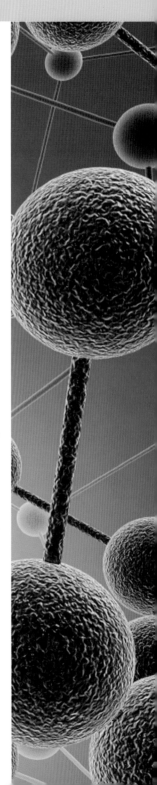

Bailey, R. A., and Don Rittner. *Encyclopedia of Chemistry*. New York, NY: Facts on File, 2005.

Barrett, Jack. *Atomic Structure and Periodicity*. Hoboken, NJ: Wiley, 2002.

Ford, Kenneth William. *The Quantum World: Quantum Physics for Everyone*. Cambridge, MA: Harvard University Press, 2004.

Gillis, H. P., Norman H. Nachtrieb, and David W. Oxtoby. *Principles of Modern Chemistry*. Fort Worth, TX: Saunders College Publishing, 1999.

Hawking, Stephen. *A Brief History of Time*. New York, NY: Bantam Books, 1998.

Manning, Phillip. *Atoms, Molecules, and Compounds*. New York, NY: Chelsea House, 2008.

Oxlade, Chris, Kirsteen Rogers, Corinne Stockley, and Jane Wertheim. *The Usborne Illustrated Dictionary of Chemistry*. Rev. ed. London, England: Usborne Children's Books, 2006.

Pullman, Bernard. *The Atom in the History of Human Thought*. New York, NY: Oxford University Press, 1998.

Rhodes, Richard. *The Making of the Atomic Bomb*. New York, NY: Simon & Schuster, 1986.

Smirnov, Boris M. *Physics of Atoms and Ions*. New York, NY: Springer, 2003.

Stwertka, Albert. *A Guide to the Elements*. New York, NY: Oxford University Press, 2002.

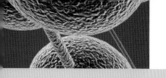

INDEX

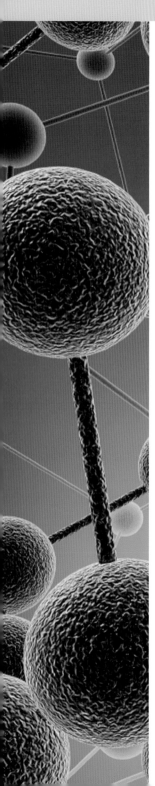

ABOUT THE AUTHOR

Joel Chaffee is a writer currently at Columbia University in New York City. An interest in the natural world caused him to further pursue knowledge in the fields of science and mathematics, swelling his reading list to include Einstein, Hawking, and, perhaps most helpfully, children's books. With attention to simple explanations for complex ideas, he hopes this title will expand the knowledge of and interest in the sciences to young readers.

PHOTO CREDITS

Cover (top), pp. 1, 54, 56, 59, 61, 62 © www.istockphoto.com/ Kasia Biel; cover (bottom) © www.istockphoto.com/Karl Dolenc; cover (back), pp. 3, 8,17, 26, 37, 45 © www.istockphoto.com/ DSGpro; pp. 8, 17, 26, 37, 45 © www.istockphoto.com/Sebastian Kaulitzki; p. 4–5 © Dr. Mitsuo Ohtsuki/Photo Researchers, Inc.; p. 9 U.S. Department of Energy, Oak Ridge National Laboratory; pp. 10–11 © ArSciMed/Photo Researchers, Inc.; pp. 13, 23, 33 Tahara Anderson; p. 18 © www.istockphoto.com/Donald Erickson; p. 20 Comstock/Getty Images; p. 27 Scala/Art Resource, NY; pp. 30–31 © Science and Society/SuperStock; pp. 34–35 Spike Mafford/Photodisc/Thinkstock; p. 38 http://mynasadata.larc. nasa.gov/images/EM_Spectrum3-new.jpg; p. 40 Topical Press Agency/Getty Images; p. 43 Imagno/Getty Images; p. 46 www. iStockphoto.com/Thinkstock; p. 48 http://en.wikipedia.org/wiki/ Nuclear_fission; p. 51 Seergei Supinsky/AFP/Getty Images.

Designer: Sam Zavieh; Editor: Nicholas Croce;
Photo Researcher: Amy Feinberg